# Lucia Di Lammermoor

# LUCIA

## DI LAMMERMOOR.

### DI SALVATORE CAMMERANO.

O

# LUCY OF LAMMERMOOR,

A TRAGIC OPERA

In Three Acts,

THE MUSIC BY DONIZETTI,

AS REPRESENTED

## AT PALMO'S NEW YORK OPERA HOUSE,

JANUARY, 1847

---

NEW YORK:

PIERCY & HOUEL, PRINTERS, 111 NASSAU STREET.
SOLD AT PALMO'S OPERA HOUSE.

[PRICE, THREE SHILLINGS.]

1847.

# PERSONAGGI

LORD ENRICO ASHTON, . Sig. Beneventano.

Miss LUCIA, *di lui sorella,* . . . Signa. Babili

SIR EDGARDO, *di Ravenswood,* Sig. Benedetti.

LORD ARTURO *Bucklaw,* . , . Sig. Benetti.

RAIMONDO BIDEBENT,⎫
  *Educatore e Confidente* ⎬ . . Sig. Martini.
  *di Lucia,* ⎭

ALISA,*damigella di Lucia,* . . Sigra. Boulard.

NORMANDO, *Capo degli* ⎫ . . . : Sig. N. N.
  *Armigeri di Ravenswood* ⎭

Dame e Cavalieri, congiunti di Ashton,
Abitanti di Lammermoor.
Paggi, Armigeri, Domestici di Ashton.

N. B.—Il soggetto di quest Opera e cosè ben descritto nella Novella di Sir Gualterio Scott, nota a tutti, che si è creduto inutile i'appoovi il solito Argomento.

L'avvenimento ha luogo in Iscozia, parte nel Castello di Ravenswood, parte nella rovinata Torre di Wotferag.

L'epoca rimonta al declinare del secolo XVI.

ENTERED according to the Act of Congress, in the year 1846, by
JOSEPH ATTINELLI,
In the Clerk's Office of the District Court, for the Southern District of New York

# DRAMATIS PERSONÆ.

LORD HENRY ASHTON, . Sig. BENEVENTANO.

Miss LUCY, *his Sister*, . . . . Signa. BARILI.

SIR EDGAR RAVENSWOOD, Sig. BENEDETTI.

LORD ARTHUR BUCKLAW, . . Sig. BENETTI.

RAYMOND BIDE-THE BENT, *Tutor and Confidant to Lucy*, . . . Sig. MARTINI.

ALICE, *Lucy's Attendant*, . . Sigra. BOULARD.

NORMAN, *Chief of the Soldiers of Ravenswood*, . . Sig. N. N.

Chorus of Ladies and Knights, relatives of Ashton, Inhabitants of Lammermoor, Pages, Soldiers, and Servants of Ashton.

N. C.—The plot of this Opera is so masterly described in the beautiful Novel by Sir Walter Scott, well known to every reader, that it has been thought useless to prefix the customary Argument.

The action lies in Scotland, near the Castle of Ravenswood, and a part in the ruined Tower of Wolf's Crag.

The Epoch towards the close of the Sixteenth Century.

# ATTO PRIMO.

## LA PARTENZA.

### SCENA PRIMA.

*Parco, con avanzi della fontana Sirena.*

NORMANNO, *Coro.*

Percorrete
  Percorriamo   le spiagge vicine
Della torre le vaste rovine :
Cada il vel di sì turpe mistero,
Lo domanda...lo impone l' onor
Fia che splenda il terribile vero
Come lampo fra nubi d' orror !    *(Il Coro parte)*

### SCENA II.

ENRICO, RAIMONDO *e detto.*

Nor.   Tu sei turbato ?
Enr.         E n' ho ben donde.   Il sai
Del mio destin sì ottenebrò la stella...
Intanto Edgardo...quel mortal nemico
Di mia prosapia, dalle sue rovine
Erge la fronte baldanzosa e ride !
Sola una mano raffermar mi puote
Nel vacillante mio poter...Lucia
Osa respinger quella mano !   Ah ! suora
Non m' è colei !

# ACT FIRST.

---

## THE DEPARTURE.

---

### SCENE FIRST.

*A Park, with the Ruins of the fountain of the Syren.*

NORMAN *and Chorus.*

Survey
   Let us explore } the neighboring shore
And the vast ruins of the tower ;
Down with the veil of a mystery so dire ;
Honor demands, honor requires it.
May the dreaded truth flash
   Like lightning amidst the gloomy clouds.
          *(exit Cho.)*

### SCENE II.

HENRY, RAYMOND, *and Chorus.*

NOR.  Thou seem'st disturbed ?
HEN.  And well I may be so !
Thou knowest that the star
Of my destiny was clouded; while Edgar,
That mortal enemy of my race,
Rises from his ruin a smiling, audacious brow.
That only hand which might sustain
My tottering power, I pray in vain
That very hand Lucy dares reject.
Ah ! no sister is she of mine.
    1*

**RAI.**            Dolente
Vergin, che geme sull' urna recente
Di cara madre, al talamo potria
Volger lo sguardo ? Ah ! rispettiam quel core,
Che per troppo dolor non sente amore.

**NOB.**   Non sente amor ! Lucia
D'amore avvampa.

**ENR.**               Che favelli ?

**RAI.**                       (Oh detto !)

**NOB.**   M' udite. Ella sen gia, colà del parco
Nel solingo vial, dove la madre
Giace sepolta ; la sua fida Alisa
Era al suo fianco. Impetuoso toro
Ecco su lor si avventa...
Prive d' ogni soccorso,
Pende sovr' esse inevitabil morte !
Quando per l' aere sibilar si sente
Un colpo, e al suol repente
Cade la belva.

**ENR.**       E chi vibrò quel colpo?

**NOB.**   Tal...che il suo nome ricoprì d'un velo

**ENR.**   Lucia forse ?

**NOB.**         L' amò.

**ENR.**             Dunque il rivide ?

**NOB.**   Ogni alba.

**ENR.**        E dove ?

**NOB.**           In quel viale.

**ENR.**               Io fremo !
Nè tu scovristi il seduttor ?

**NOB.**                Sospetto.
In n' ho soltanto.

**ENR.**       Ah ! parla.

**NOB.**   E tuo nemico.

**RAI.**      (Oh ciel !)

**NOB.**           Tu lo detesti.

**ENR.**   Esser potrebbe ! Edgardo ?

**RAI.**          Ah !

**NOB.**            Lo dicesti...

**Ray.** Can a mourning virgin,
Who weeps o'er a dear mother's recent tomb,
Bend her thoughts on nuptials ?
Ah ! let us respect a grieving heart,
Which oppressed with sorrow,
Is not stained with love.

**Nor.** Not stained with !
Lucy consumes with love.

**Hen.** What sayest thou ?

**Ray.** (What words !)

**Nor.** Listen to me—is known to thee
Yon solitary walk in the park,
Wich leads to her mother's grave ;
Accompanied by her faithful Alice,
She there bent her steps,
When suddenly an impetuous bull
Rushed on them.   Far from help,
An inevitable death seemed pending
O'er their days—on a sudden a sound pierced
And lifeless fell the animal to earth. [the air,

**Hen.** Who darted the blow ?

**Nor.** One who veiled his name in mystery.

**Hen.** Lucy perhaps—

**Nor.** Loved him !

**Hen.** Then they met again ?

**Nor.** At each dawn of day

**Hen.** Where ?—

**Nor.** In that same walk.

**Hen.** I tremble.
Hast thou not discovered the seducer ?

**Nor.** Suspicion *is* all I have.

**Hen.** Speak, ah ! speak !

**Nor.** 'Tis thine enemy.

**Rev.** (Oh Heaven !)

**Nor.** He is hateful to thee.

**Hen.** Can it be ?   Edgar ?

**Ray.** Ah !

**Nor.** Thou hast named him.

ENR.   Cruda...funesta smania
Tu m' hai destata in petto!
E' troppo, e troppo orribile
Questo fatal sospetto!
Mi fa gelare e fremere!
Mi drizza in fronte il crin!
Colma di tanto obbrobrio
Chi suora mia nascea!—
Pria che d'amor sì perfido
A me svelarti rea,
Se ti colpisse un fulmine,
Fora men rio destin

NOR.   Pietoso al tuo decoro,
Io fui con te crudel!

RAI.   (La tua clemenza imploro:
Tu lo smentisci, o ciel.)

## SCENA III.

*Coro di cacciatori e detti.*

Coro.     Il tuo dubbio è mai certezza.
NOR.   Odi tu?
ENR.    Narrate.
RAI.      (Oh giorno!)
Coro.   Come vinti da stanchezza,
Dopo lungo errar d' intorno,
Noi posammo della torre
Nel vestibulo cadente:
Ecco tosto lo trascorre
Un uom pallido e tacente.
Quando appresso ei n' è venuto.
Ravvisiam lo sconosciuto.
Ei su celere destriero
S' involò dal nostro sguardo
Ci fe' noto un falconiero
Il suo nome.

ENR.       E quale?
Coro.        Edgardo.

HEN. A cruel and fatal phrenzy
   Hast thou given birth to in my heart—
   So horrid and so terrible
   Is this suspicion that I
   Shudder and tremble now;
   My hair stands erect upon my brow.
  Thus stained with dishonor
   Is she who whom I called my sister;
   Less adverse would have been my fate
   Had a thunderbolt fallen on thee,
   Ere thou wert guilty
   Of this perfidious love.

NOR. Jealous of thy honor made me
   Be thus cruel to thee!

RAY. (I implore, oh Heaven, grant
   That his words may yet prove false.)

## SCENE III.

*Chorus of Huntsmen and the above.*

Cho. Thy doubts are now confirmed.
NOR. Dost thou hear it?
HEN. Relate.
RAY. (Oh fatal day!)
Cho. After long wanderings
   Oppressed and fatigued
   We reposed in the ruined
   Vestibule of the tower,
   A pallid and silent stranger
   Suddenly crossed there:
   But as he was drawing near
   We recognised the unknown,
   But a rapid courser soon
   Bore him from our sight;
   A falconer revealed
   To us his name.
HEN. What is it?
Cho. Edgar!

ENR.     Egli!  Oh rabbia che m' accendi,
          Contenerti un cor non può!
RAI.     Ah! non credere...ah! sospendi...
          Ella...M' odi...
ENR.                 Udir non vo
          La pietade in suo favore
          Miti sensi invan ti delta...
          Se mi parli di vendetta
          Solo intender ti potrò.—
          Sciagurati! il mio furore
          Già su voi tremendo rugge...
          L' empia fiamma che vi strugge
          Io col sangue spegnerò.
NOR. *Coro* Quell' indeguo al nuovo albore
          L'ira tua fuggir non può.
RAI.     (Ahi! qual nembo di terrore
          Questa casa circondò!)
             (ENRICO *parte: tutto lo seguono.*)


## SCENA IV.

### LUCIA *ed* ALISA.

LUC.     Ancor non giunse!
ALI.           Incauta! a che mi traggi!
          Avventurarti, or che il fratel quì venne,
          E' folle ardir.
LUC.           Ben parli! Edgardo sappia
          Qual ne minaccia orribile periglio...
ALI.     Perchè d'intorno il ciglio
          Volgi atterrita?
LUC.                Quella fonte mai.
          Senza tremar, non veggo. Ah! tu lo sai.
          Un Ravenswood, ardendo
          Di geloso furor, l' amata donna
          Colà trafisse: l' infelice cadde
          Nell' onda, ed ivi rimanea sepolta...
          M' apparve l' ombra sua.
ALI                 Che intendo!

HEN.    Him! This heart cannot command
The rage which consumes it.
RAY. Ah! Believe it not. Suspend
Thy judgment. She—hear me—
HEN.                 I will not listen,
In vain does pity in his favor plead,
And inspire me with soft emotions—
Nought I'll hear—none shall speak
But the voice of vengeance.
Perfidious ones! My anger
Already fearful bursts on you,
And with your blood I'll extinguish
The guilty flame which consumes ye.
NOR. *and Cor.* At dawn of day the guilty one
Cannot escape thy fury—
RAY. (Ah! what a cloud of horror
Surrounds this house!)


## SCENE IV.

### LUCY *and* ALICE

LUCY   He is not yet arrived.
ALI.           Uncautious one, what seekest thou,
The risk is great, thy brother has been here,
Just now. 'Tis madness.
LUCY         True, Edgard shall know
By what horrible peril we are threatened.
ALI.   Why thus seized by fear,
Dost thou look around.
LUCY         I never behold
That fountain without dread. Know
That one Ravenswood, whom jealousy
Had made mad, his beloved
Murdered there. The unhappy one
Fell in that water, and had her tomb there,
But her shadow did appear.
ALI.         What do I hear.

Luc.                                                      Ascolta !
Regnava nel silenzio
    Alta la notte e bruna...
    Colpia la fonte un pallido
    Raggio di tetra luna...
    Quando sommesso gemito
    Fra l' aure udir si fè,
Ed ecco su quel margine
    L' ombra mostrarsi a me !
Qual di chi parla muoversi
    Il labbro suo vedea,
    E con la mano esanime
    Chiamarmi a se parea.
    Stette un momento immobile
    Poi rapida sgombrò,
E l' onda pria si limpida,
    Di sangue rosseggiò !—

Ali.                Chiari, oh ciel ! ben chiari e tristi
Nel tuo dir presagi intendo !
Ah ! Lucia, Lucia desisti
Da un amor così tremendo.

Luc.                Io ?.. che parli !   Al cor che geme
    Quest' affetto è sola speme
    Senza Edgardo non potrei
    Un' istante respirar...
Egli è luce a' giorni miei,
    E conforto al mio penar.
    Quando rapito in estasi
    Del più cocente amore,
    Col favellar del core
    Mi giura eterna fè :
Gli affanni miei dimentico
    Gioja diviene il pianto...
    Parmi che a lui' d' accanto
    Si schiuda il ciel per me !

Ali.            Giorni di amaro pianto
    Si apprestano per te !
Egli s' avanza... La vicina soglia
Io cauta veglierò.      (*Rientra nel castello*)

LUCY                      Listen to me :
Dreary and sad was the awful night ;
   Silence all over prevailed.
   A pale beam faintly spread
   The veiled moon, on the fount,
   When a groan, heavily subdued,
   In the still air, was heard.
And lo, on that very fount
   The shadow appeared to me,
And as a living mortal
   His lips move I could see,
   And then with the bloodless hand
   Appeared to call for me,
   Remained still for for a moment,
   Then swiftly off it went,
And that water so limped before
   Was tinged with gore.

ALI.       Heavens, too mournful, and still too clear
Are thy words, by which misfortunes I fore-
   Lucy, Lucy, stop, refrain        [see.
   From so dreadful, awful, love.

LUCY    I! what sayst thou, the grieving heart
   Has no other life nor hope.
   I could not live, one instant more,
   Should I ever from Edgar part.
He is of my days, the only light
   To my sorrows, my only delight.
   When as if in ecstacy raptured
   By the most burning love,
   Speaking with all his heart,
   Swears to me, eternal faith.
My sorrows I forget ;
   My tears turn into joy,
   By him, methinks I see
   The Heavens open for me.

ALI.    Alas ! what days full of tears
      Await thee. I fear
He comes hither ; I will cautiously
Watch the adjoining castle.
     2

## SCENA V.

EDGARDO, *e detta.*

EDG.
      Lucia, perdona
Se ad ora inusitata
Io vederti chiedea: ragion possente
A ciò mi trasse. Pria che in ciel biancheggi
L' alba novella; dalle patrie sponde
Lungi sarò.

LUC.
      Che dici!

EDG.
Pe' franchi lidi amici
Sciolgo le vele; ivi trattar m' è dato
Le sorti della Scozia. Il mio cognato:
Athol. Riparator di mie sciagure,
A tanto onor m' innalza

LUC.
      E me nel pianto
Abbandoni così!

EDG.
      Pria di lasciarti
Ashton mi vegga... stenderò placato
A lui la destra, e la tua destra, pegno
Fra noi di pace, chiederò.

LUC.
      Che ascolto !..
Ah ! no... rimanga nel silenzio avvolto
Per or l' arcano affetto

EDG.
      Intendo !—Di mia stirpe
Il reo persecutore
Ancor pago non é ? Mi tolse il padre...
Il mio retaggio avito
Con trame inique m' usurpò... Nè basta ?
Che brama ancor ? che chiede
Quel cor feroce, e rio ?
La mia perdita intera, il sangue mio ?
Ei mi abborre...

LUC.
      Ah ! no...

EDG.
      Mi abborre...

LUC.
Calma, oh ciel ! quell' ira estrema

EDG.
Fiamma ardente in sen mi scorre.
M' odi.

LUC.
    Edgardo !

## SCENA V.

### Edgar *and* Lucy.

Edg.                    Lucy, forgive me,
If, at this unusual hour,
I sought to see thee, but a potent reason
Is the cause.   Before the rising dawn
Illumines the heavens, I shall be far
From my native shore.

Lucy.                    What sayest thou ?

Edg.  For the friendly shores of France,
Unfurling are the sails, and there
I am to treat on Scotland's destiny.   [wrongs,
Athol, my relative, and the redresser of my
'Tis to him I owe this post of honor.

Lucy.                    And canst thou thus
Abandon me to grief ?

Edg.                    Ere I quit thee,
Ashton shall see me ; to him I'll offer
A friendly hand, and ask thine in return,
As a pledge of peace between us.

Lucy.                    What do I hear ?
Ah, no ! let our secret love yet remain
Silently veiled in mystery.

Edg.                    I understand thee,
The guilty persecutor of my house
Is not yet appeased; he robbed me of my
Usurped the inheritance of my family  [father
By treacherous schemes---and is this not
What desires he more ?            [enough ?
What does that base, ferocious heart pretend ?
My blood—my utter ruin—
He abhors me !

Lucy.              Ah, no !

Edg.              He hates me !

Lucy.    Oh, Heaven ! Calm thy anger.

Edg.    An ardent flame burns in this bosom ;
Listen !

Lucy.              Edgar ?

Eng.         M' odi, e trema
  Sulla tomba che rinserra
   Il tradito genitore,
   Al tuo sangue eterna guerra
   Io giurai nel mio furore :
   Ma ti vidi... in cor mi nacque...
   Altro affetto, e l' ira tacque...
   Pur quel voto non è infranto...
   Io potrei compirlo ancor !
Luc. Deh ! ti placa... deh ! ti frena..
   Può tradirne un solo accento !
   Non ti basta la mia pena ?
   Vuoi ch' io muoja di spavento ?
   Ceda, ceda ogn' altro affetto :
   Solo amor t' infiammi il petto...
   Ah ! il più nobile il più santo
   De' tuoi voti è un puro amor !
Eng. Quì di sposa eterna fede
   Quì mi giura, al cielo innante.
   Dio ci ascolta, Dio ci vede....
   Tempio ed ara è un core amante
   Al tuo fato unisco il mio.
   Son tuo sposo.
Luc.      E tua son io.
   A' miei voti amore invoco.
Eng. A' miei voti invoeo il ciel
Luc. Eng. Porrà fine al nostro foco
   Sol di morte il freddo gel.
Eng. Separarci ormai conviene.
Luc. Oh parola a me funesta !
   Il mio cor con te ne viene
Eng. Il mio cor con te quì resta.
Luc. Ah ! talor del tuo pensiero
   Venga un foglio messaggiero,
   E la vita fuggitiva
   Di speranza nutrirò.
Eng. Io di te memoria viva
   Sempre, o cara serberò.

EDG.                              Hear me, and tremble.
On the tomb which encloses
    The betrayed ashes of my father,
    I, in my wrath, swore
    To thy race an eternal war—
    But I saw thee, another passion
    Rose in my breast, and hushed my anger ;
    Yet my vow is not broken.
    I may yet fulfil it !
LUCY.   Alas ! be calm, moderate thy anger,
    One accent may betray us ;
    Does not my grief suffice thee ?
    Wilt thou see me die with fear ?
    Let all other passions yield,
    Love only should invade thy heart.
    Ah ! the noblest, the holiest of all thy vows
    Is a chaste, a pure love !
EDG.    Swear, swear here to me,
    In the face of heaven, an eternal faith—
    God hears us, God sees us ;
    A loving heart is both temple and altar.
    To thy fate I unite mine ;
    I am thy consort.
LUCY.                              And I am thine.
    Love I invoke as witness to my vows.
EDG.    And Heaven I invoke to mine.
EDG. & LUCY. The icy hand of death alone
    Shall end our love.
EDG.    We must now part.
LUCY.   Oh ! fatal word to me !
    My heart will follow thee.
EDG.    And with thee will mine remain.
LUCY.   Alas ! at least let me receive
    Thy letters, companions of thy thoughts :
    So shall hope feed
    My anxious life.
EDG.    An eternal memory of thee
    I'll unceasingly preserve.
                        *2

Luc. Edg. Verranno a te sull' aura
      I miei sospiri ardenti,
      Udrai nel mar che mormora
      L'eco de' miei lamenti
        Pensando eh' io di gemiti
        Mi pasco, e di dolor.
      Spargi una mesta lagrima
        Su questo pegno allor.

Edg.     Io parto...
Lub.           Addio..
Erg.               Rammentati!
    Ne stringe il cielo!
Luc.               E amor.

FINE DELL' ATTO PRIMO.

Lucy & Edg. The zephyrs will waft to thee
        My ardent sighs,
        And, blended with the murmuring sea,
        Thou wilt hear an echo to my woes:
            Think then that on sighs
            And grief I live,
        And on this pledge
            Shed a mournful tear.

Edg.        I must away !
Lucy.                    Adieu !
Edg.                                Remember,
        Heaven united us !
Lucy.                            And also Love.


END OF THE FIRST ACT.

# ATTO SECONDO.

## IL CONTRATTO NUZIALE.

### SCENA PRIMA.

*Gabinetto negli appartamenti di Lord Asthon.*

#### ENRICO e NORMANNO.

NOR. Lucia fra poco a te verrà.

ENR.       Tremante
L' aspetto.   A festeggiar le nozze illustri
Già nel castello i nobili congiunti
Di mia famiglia accolsi, in breve Arturo
Quì volge—E s' ella pertinace osasse
D'opporsi?

NOR.     Non temer : la lunga assenza
Del tuo nemico, i fogli
Da noi rapiti, e la bugiarda nuova
Ch'egli s'accese d'altra fiamma, in core
Di Lucia spegneranno il cieco amore.

ENR. Ella s'avanza !   Il simulato foglio
Porgimi, ed esci sulla via che tragge
Alla città regina
Di Scozia ; e qui fra plausi, e liete grida
Conduci Arturo.      (NOR. *parte.*

### SCENA II.

#### LUCIA, e *detto.*

ENR.    Appressati, Lucia.
Sperai più lieta in questo dì vederti,
In questo dì, che d'imeneo le faci
Si accendono per te.—Mi guardi, e taci ?

# ACT SECOND.

## THE NUPTIAL AGREEMENT.

### SCENE FIRST.

*A Cabinet in Lord Ashton's house.*

HENRY *and* NORMAN.

NOR. Lucy will ere long be here.
HEN. With a trembling heart I wait her.
To celebrate the illustrious nuptials,
Already in the castle are assembled
My noble relatives. To be brief, Arthur
Will soon be here, and if obstinately
She should dare oppose ?
NOR. Fear not—the lengthened absence
Of thy enemy, the intercepted letters,
And the circulated falsehood,
That he burns, with another flame, will soon,
In Lucy's heart, extinguish her blind love.
HEN. Here she comes ! Give me
The forged writing. Go upon the road
Which leads to Scotland's royal city ;
There, amidst festive sounds and joyful homage
Conduct here Arthur. - (*exit* NOR.)

### SCENE II.

HENRY *aud* LUCY.

HEN. Draw near Lucy. I hope
To behold thee to-day more gay and smiling :
On this day, when Hymen's torch is lighting
Thou lookest at me and art silent. [for thee.

|          |                                              |
|----------|----------------------------------------------|
| Luc.     | Il pallor funesto, orrendo                   |
|          | Che ricopre il volto mio,                    |
|          | Ti rimproverà tacendo                        |
|          | Il mio strazio.... il mio dolor.             |
|          | Perdonar ti possa Iddio                      |
|          | L'inumano tuo rigor.                         |
| Enr.     | A ragion mi fè spietato                      |
|          | Quel che t'arse indegno affetto...           |
|          | Ma si taccia del passato...                  |
|          | Tuo fratello io sono ancor.                  |
|          | Spenta è l'ira nel mio petto,                |
|          | Spegni tu l'insano amor.                     |
| Luc.     | La pietade è tarda omai!                      |
|          | Il mio fin di già s'appressa.                |
| Enr.     | Viver lieta ancor potrai...                  |
| Luc.     | Lieta! e puoi tu dirlio a me?                 |
| Enr.     | Nobil sposo...                               |
| Luc.     | Cessa....ah! cessa.                          |
|          | Ad altr'uomo giurai la fè                    |
| Enr.     | Nol potevi....                               |
| Luc.     | Enrico!                                      |
| Enr.     | Or basti                                     |
|          | Questo foglio appien ti dice,                |
|          | Qual crudel, qual empio amasti.              |
|          | Leggi.                                       |
| Luc.     | Il core mi balzò!                            |
| Enr.     | Tu vacilli!                                  |
| Luc.     | Me infelice!                                 |
|          | Ahi! la folgore piombò!                      |
|          | Soffriva nel pianto....languia nel dolore... |
|          | La speme....la vita riposi in un core....    |
|          | Quel core infedele ad altra si diè!          |
|          | L'istante di morte è giunto per me.          |
| Enr.     | Un folle ti accese, un perfido amore;        |
|          | Tradisti il tuo sangue per vil seduttore     |
|          | Ma degna dal cielo ne avesti mercè:          |
|          | Quel core infedele ad altra si diè!          |

LUCY | This fatal and horrid paleness
Which o'erspread my face,
Reproaches thee silently
With all my woes and anguish.
May God pardon thee
Thy inhuman rigor.

HEN. The worthless flame thou hast cherished
Gave me a claim to abandon pity;
But no more of past events.
I am yet thy brother;
Anger has fled this bosom;
May it be the same with thy love.

LUCY Thy pity comes too late;
Already my end approaches.

HEN. You may yet live happy.

LUCY Happy! and canst thou speak thus to me?

HEN. A noble consort!

LUCY Cease—ah cease!
To another I've pledged my faith.

HEN. Thou could'st not.

LUCY Henry!

HEN. Enough;
This writing will inform thee better
Of the cruel and impious man
Thou hast so much loved; read.

LUCY My heart palpitates.

ENR. Thou tremblest!

LUCY Ah wretched me!
A thunderbolt has fallen on me. '
I pined in tears and anguish,
And on one heart reposed hope and life;
That faithless heart is given to another;
The hour of death is come for me.

HEN. A rash and perfidious heart inflamed thee;
Thy blood thou hast betrayed for a vile
[seducer.
But worthy of heaven is the reward thou
[hast received;
That treacherous heart is now another's.

Luc.    Che fia !

Enr.          Suonar di giubbilo
Senti la riva ?

Luc.         Ebbene ?

Enr.   Giunge il tuo sposo.

Luc.           Un brivido
Mi corse per le vene !

Enr.   A te s'appressa il talamo....

Luc.   La tomba a me s'appresta !

Enr.   Ora fatale è questa !
M'odi.

Luc.        Mi copre gli occhi un vel !

Enr.   Spento è Guglielmo....a Scozia
Comanderà Maria....
Prostrata è nella polvere
La parte ch'io seguia....

Luc.   Tremo !

Enr.        Dal precipizio
Arturo può sottrarmi,
Sol egli...

Luc.       Ed io ?...

Eur.        Salvarmi
Devi.

Luc.     Ma !...

Eur.      Il devi.

Luc.          Oh ciel !

Enr.   Se tradirmi tu potrai,
La mia sorte è già compita...
Tu m'involi onore, e vita ;
Tu la scure appresti a me...
Ne' tuoi sogni mi vedrai.
Ombra irata e minacciosa !
Quella scure sanguinosa
Starà sempre innanzi a te !

Luc.   Tu che vedi il pianto mio...
Tu che leggi in questo core,
Se respinto il mio dolore
Come in terra in cièl non è.

LUCY    What noise is that?

HEN.          Dost hear the shore resound
With festive sounds?

LUCY          Well!

HEN.    Thy consort comes!

LUCY          A cold shivering
Flows through my veins.

HEN.    Thy nuptials are preparing.

LUCY    My tomb, thou mean'st.

HEN.    This is the fatal moment.
Listen.

LUCY    A mist is o'er my eyes.

HEN.    In his tomb lies William.
On the throne Mary will ascend
Ruined is the party
Which I followed.

LUCY    I tremble.

HEN.    Arthur can alone save me
From the precipice;
Him only.

LUCY          And I?

HEN.    Thou ought to save me.
Thou shalt.

LUCY       But—

HEN.          Thou must.

LUCY          Oh heaven!

HEN.          If thou betrayest me.
My fate is sealed;
Prepared by thee will be that axe,
Which must deprive me of honor and life;
In thy dreams ever present
Will be my angry menacing shade,
And before thee
That blood-stained axe will be.

LUCY    Oh God! thou see'st my tears,
And can read my inmost heart;
If my grief is not despised
In heaven, as it is on earth,

Tu mi togli, eterno Iddio
Questa vita disperata...
Io son tanto sventurata,
Che la morte è un ben per me!

## SCENA III.

ENRICO, ARTURO, NORMANNO, *Cavalieri e Dame Con-
giunti di* ASHTON, *paggi, Armigeri, Abitanti di Lam-
mermoor, e Domestici.*

ENR. NOR. *Coro.*

Per te d'immenso giubbilo
Tutto s'avviva intorno,
Per te veggiam rinascere
Della speranza il giorno.
Quì l'amistà ti guida,
Quì ti conduce amor,
Qual'astro in notte infida,
Qual riso nel dolor.

ART. Per poco fra le tenebre
Sparì la vostra stella,
Io la farò risorgere
Più fulgida e più bella.
La man mi porgi Enrico...
Ti stringi a questo cor.
A te ne vengo; amico,
Fratello, e difensor.
Dov'é Lucia?

ENR.    Quì giungere
Or la vedrem...Se in lei
Soverchia è la mestizia,
Maravigliar non dei
Dal duolo oppressa e vinta
Piange la madre estinta...

ART. M' é noto.—Or solvi un dubbio
Fama suonò, ch'Edgardo
Sovr'essa temerario
Alzare osò lo sguardo...

Take to Thee, eternal God,
This disparing life,
For death will be a reprieve
To woe so great.

### SCENE III.

HENRY, ARTHUR, NORMAN, *Knights and Ladies, relatives of* ASHTON, *Pages and Soldiers, and inhabitants of Lammermoor.*

HENRY, NORMAN, *and Chorus.*

All around is animated
  With unbounded joy;
  For thee we see revive
  A day of hope;
  Friendship guides thee hither;
  Love leads thee here,
Like a star in a cloudy night;
  Like a smile amidst tears.

ART.   Your star has disappeared
  But as if by a passing cloud obscured,
  I will cause it again to rise
  With greater beauty and splendor.
  Henry give me thy hand.
  Embrace me, come to my heart
  I come to thee as faithful friend,
  As brother, as defender.
  But where is Lucy?

HEN.             She'll soon appear!
  Be not surprised
  To see her plunged in gloom.
  She mourns her mother's death
  Grief seems to conquer her
  And take her mind away.

ART.   I know it. Now solve a doubt;
  Report says that Edgar
  Dared rashly cast
  On her an audacious look.

Enr.  E ver...quel folle ardir...

Nob. *Coro.* S'avanza a te Lucia.

## SCENA IV.

LUCIA, ALISA, RAIMONDO, *e detti*

Enr.  Ecco il tuo sposo.. Incauta !
    Perder mi vuoi ?

Luc.      (Gran Dio.)

Art.  Ti piaccia i voti accogliere
    Del tenero amor mio...

Art.    Oh dolce invito!

Luc.  (Io vado al sacrifizio!)

Rai.  (Reggi buon Dio l'afflitta.)

Enr.  Non esitar.

Luc.   Me misera !
  La mia condanna ho scritta !)

Enr.  (Respiro !)

Luc.     (Io gelo ed ardo !
  Io manco !)

*Tutti.*   Qual fragor !
  Chi giunge ?

## SCENA V.

EDGARDO, *alcuni servi, e detti.*

Edg. Edgardo.

*Gli altri.*    Edgardo !

Luc.  Oh fulmine...

*Tutti.* Oh, terror !

Enr. (Chi rattiene il mio furore,
  E la man che al brando corse ?
  Della misera in favore
  Nel mio petto un gido sorse
  E mio sangue ! io l'ho tradita !
  Ella sta fra morte e vita !
  Ah ! che spegnere non posso
  Un rimorso nel mio cor !

Edg. (Chi mi frena in tal momento !
  Chi troncò dell'ire il corso ?

Hen.     'Tis true, that senseless men dared—
Nor. & Cho. Here Lucy comes!

## SCENE IV.

Lucy, Alice, Raymond, and the above.

Hen.    Behold thy consort!—(Rash one,
        Wilt thou ruin me?)
Lucy   (Great God!)
Art.    Deign to accept the homage
        Of an ardent love.
Art.    Oh, dear invitation!
Lucy   (I am going to be sacrificed.)
Ray.   (Support, O God, the afflicted one!)
Hen.    No hesitation.
Lucy   (Ah, wretched me!
        I have sealed my doom.)
Hen.    (I breathe.)
Lucy   (I freeze and shudder,
        Strength fails me.)
All.    What tumult!—
        Who comes?

## SCENE V.

Edgar, Domestics, and the above.

Edg.   Edgar.
Others. Edgar!
Lucy.  Oh, thunderbolt!
All.    Oh, terror!
Hen.    (Who stays my anger,
        And arrests the hand which seeks my sword?
        In favour of the unhappy one
        A voice speaks to my soul.
        'Tis my blood,—I have betrayed her!
        She is between life and death!
        Ah, why cannot I hush remorse,
        Which rises in my heart?)
Edg.   (Who holds me in such a moment?
        Who stems the current of my anger?
        3*

Il suo duolo il suo spavento
Son la pruova d'un rimorso!
Ma, qual rosa inaridita,
Ella sta fra morte e vita!
Io son vinto....son commosso ...
T'amo, ingrata, t'amo ancor!)

Luc.    Io sperai che a me la vita
Tronca avesse il mio spavento....
Ma la morte non m'aita.....
Vivo ancor per mio tormento!—
Da'miei lumi cadde il velo....
Mi tradì la terra e il cielo!
Vorrei pianger ma non posso....
Ah! mi manca il pianto ancor!)

Art. Rai. Ali. Norm. *Coro.*

(Qual terribile momento!
Più formar non so parole!
Densa nube di spavento
Par che copra i rai del sole!—
Come rosa inaridita
Ella sta fra morte e vita!
Chi per lei non è commosso
Ha di tigre in petto il cor.)

Enr. Art. Nor.*Caval.*

Ti allontana, sciagurato....
O il tuo sangue fia versato....

Edg.    Morirò, ma insiem col mio
Altro sangue scorrerà.

Rai.    Rispettate, o voi, di Dio
La tremenda maestà.
In suo nome io vel comando,
Deponete l'ira e il brando.
Pace pace....egli abborrisce
L'omicida, e scritto sta:
Chi di ferro altrui ferisce,
Pur di ferro perirà.

Enr.    Ravenswood in queste porte.
Chi ti guida?

Her grief and fears
Are proofs of her remorse;
But like a withered rose
She stands between life and death.
I am moved—I am conquered—
I love thee, ungrateful one—I love thee still.)

LUCY (With fear I hoped
My life to have ceased,
But death comes not to my aid;
I live still for woe;
Now falls the veil from before my eyes;
Heaven and earth have betrayed me!
I would weep, but cannot;
Ah, even tears are denied me.)

ARTHUR, RAYMOND, ALICE, NORMAN, *and Chorus*.

(What a fatal moment!—
Words in vain I seek—
The sun's rays seem wrapped
In clouds of fear and dread.
She is like a withered rose
Between life and death;
He who feels not compassion for her,
In his bosom holds a tiger's heart.)

HENRY, ARTHUR, NORMAN, *and Knights*.

Away, rash man,
Or shed thy blood will be!

EDG. I shall die; but others' blood
With mine spilt shall be!

RAY. Respect the terrible
Majesty of God;
In his name I command it!
Depose your sword and anger!
Peace, peace; homicide he abhors;
And it is written,
That who strikes with the sword,
By the sword shall perish.

HEN. Who led thee through the gates
Ravenswood?

Edg. La mia sorte,
  Il mio dritto...sì; Lucia
  La sua fede a me giurò.

Bal. Questo amor per sempre obblìa;
  Ella è d'altri!

Edg.       D'altri! ah! no.

Rai. Mira.

Edg.    Tremi! ti confondi?
  Son tue cifre?
   A me rispondi:
  Son tue cifre?

Luc.      Sì...

Edg.      Riprendi
  Il tuo pegno, infido cor,
  Il mio dammi.

Luc.      Almen...

Edg.       Lo rendi.
  Hai tradito il cielo, e amor!
  Maledetto sia l'istante
   Che di te mi rese amante...
   Stirpe iniqua...abbominata
   Io dovea da te fuggir!
  Ah! di Dio la mano irata
   Ti disperda...

   Enr. Art. Nor. *Cavalieri.*
   Insano ardir!

 Esci, fuggi il furor che mi/ne accende

  Solo un punto i suoi colpi sospende...
  Ma fra poco più atroce, più fiero
  Sul tuo capo abborrito cadrà...
  Sì, la macchia d'oltraggio sì nero
  Col tuo sangue lavata sarà.

Edg. Trucidatemi, e pronubo al rito
  Sia lo scempio d'un core tradito...
  Del mio sangue bagnata la soglia
  Dolce vista per l'empia sarà!
  Calpestando l'esangue mia spoglia
   All' altare più lieta ne andrà!

| | |
|---|---|
| Edg. | Fate! |
| | My right! Yes, Lucy |
| | Gave her faith to me. |
| Ray. | From henceforth forget this love;— |
| | She is now another's! |
| Edg. | Another's! Oh, no! |
| Ray. | Look! |
| Edg. | Dost thou tremble, and art confused; |
| | Are these thy characters? |
| | Answer me, |
| | Is this thine hand. |
| Lucy | Yes! |
| Edg. | Take again |
| | Thy pledge, perfidious heart, |
| | Return me mine. |
| Lucy | At least—— |
| Edg. | Give it me: |
| | Heaven and Love thou hast betrayed! |
| | I curse the moment |
| | When I gave my love to thee! |
| | Guilty and cruel race, |
| | I ought to have fled thee! |
| | Ah! may an angry God |
| | Destroy ye. |

HENRY, ASHTON, NORMAN, *and Knights.*
                Delirious boldness!

For a moment anger suspends $^{my}_{our}$ blows,
        Begone, fly;
        But ere long it will fall
        On thy detested head more terrible.
Yes, thy blood alone can wipe away
        The stain of such an outrage.

| | |
|---|---|
| Edg. | Strike! Let the sacrifice |
| | Of a betrayed heart preside at her nuptials; |
| | This threshold bathed with my blood |
| | Will be a charm for her;— |
| | More joyously to the altar will she walk, |
| | When treading my mortal remains. |

Luc.   Dio lo salva...in sì fiero momento'
      D'una misera ascolta l'accento...
      E la prece d'immenso dolore
      Che più in terra speranza non ha...
    E l'estrema domanda del core,
      Che sul labro spirando mi sta!

        Rai., All., Dame.

Infelice, t'invola...t'affretta!    (A Edgardo.)
    I tuoi giorni...il suo stato rispetta.
    Vivi...e forse il tuo duolo fia spento
    Tutto è lieve all'eterna pietà.
Quante volte ad un solo tormento
    Mille gioie succeder non fa!

FINE DELL' ATTO SECONDO.

LUCY   God in this dire moment protect him!
     Listen to the accents of an unhappy one!
     'Tis the prayer of grief
     Which has on earth no hope;—
   'Tis the last request of an expiring heart,
     Now on my lips, ready from hence to part.

      RAYMOND, ALICE, *and ladies.*

Unhappy man! Away, begone—Respect
    Thy days the grief in which she's plunged;
    Perhaps ere long thy sorrow will be calmed;
    All is possible to Eternal pity!
How often have a thousand joys
    Succeeded a moment of grief!

**END OF THE SECOND ACT.**

# ATTO TERZO.

## SCENA PRIMA.

*Luogo terreno nella Torre di Wolferag.*

Edg.  Orrida è questa notte
Come il destino mio! Sì, tuona, o cielo..
Imperversate o turbini,.. sconvolto
Sia l' ordine delle cose, e pera il mondo..
Io non m' inganno! scalpitar d' appresso
Odo un destrier !—s' arresta !
Chi mai della tempesta
Fra le minacce e l' ire
Chi puote a me venìre?

## SCENA II.

### EDGARDO *ed* ENRICO.

Enr.                        Io.
Edg.                                    Quale ardire !
Ashton !
Edg.            Sì.
Enr,              Fra queste mura
Osi offrirti al mio cospetto !
Enr.   Io vi sto per tua sciagura.
Non venìsti nel mio tetto ?
Edg.   Qui del padre ancor s' aggira
L' ombra inulta ... e par che frema
Morte ogn' aura a te quì spira.
Il terren per te quì trema !
Nel varcar la soglia orrenda
Ben dovesti palpitar.
Come un uom che vivo scenda
La sua tomba ad albergar.

# ACT THIRD.

## SCENE FIRST.

*A Room in the Castle of Wolf's Crag.*

Edg.  This night is gloomy like my fate.
Yes, thunder, O heaven !
Rage, O lightning ! may the universe
Be overthrown, and the world perish.
Am I not deceived ? The distant sound
Of an advancing steed I hear ;—
He stops—who can have braved
The fury of the tempest,
To come and find me ?

## SCENE II.

### Edgar *and* Henry.

Hen.  'Tis I !
Edg.  Audacious one !—
     Ashton !
Hen.  Yes!
Edg.            Darest thou
  In these walls present thyself ?
Hen.  For thy sorrow I am here :
  Didst thou not come under my roof?
Edg.  In this place yet wanders the unavenged
  Spirit of my father, he seems to threaten ;
  Death for thee is in every breeze ;
  The earth gapes under thy feet.
  In crossing this threshold
  Thy heart must have throbbed
Like a man who descends
  Alive into his tomb.

4

| | |
|---|---|
| ENR. | Fu condotta al sacro rito, |
| | Quindi al talamo Lucia. |
| EDG. | (Ei più squarcia il cor ferito... |
| | Oh tormento ! oh gelosia !) |
| ENR. | Di letizia il mio soggiorno |
| | E di plausi rimbombava ; |
| | Ma più forte al cor d' intorno |
| | La vendetta a me parlava. |
| | Quì mi trassi... in mezzo ai venti |
| | La sua voce udia tuttor ? |
| | E il furor degli elementi |
| | Rispondeva al mio furor ! |
| EDG. | Da me che brami ? |
| ENR. | Ascoltami : |
| | Onde punir l' offesa, |
| | De' miei la spada vindice |
| | Pende su te sospesa... |
| | Ch' altri ti spenga ?   Ah ! mai... |
| | Chi dee svenarti il sai |
| EDG. | So che al paterno cenere |
| | Giurai strapparti il core. |
| ENR. | Tu !... |
| EDG. | Quando ? |
| ENR. | Al primo sorgere |
| | Del mattutino albore. |
| EDG. | Ove ? |
| ENR. | Fra l' urne gelide |
| | Dei Ravenswood. |
| EDG. | Verrò. |
| ENR. | Ivi a restar preparati. |
| EDG. | Ivi...t' ucciderò. |

a 2

O sole, più rapido a sorger t' appresta...
Ti cinga di sangue ghirlanda funesta !
Così tu rischiara—l'orribile gara
D' un odio mortale d' un cieco furor.
Farà di nostr' alme atroce governo
Gridando vendetta, lo spirto d' Averno...

HEN.  On quitting the altar, Lucy was led
To the nuptial chamber

EDG.  (Ah! he opens anew
My heart's wounds.  Oh jealousy!)

HEN.  My dwelling resounded
With festive sounds and peals of joy,
But revenge spoke more loudly
To my grieving heart—
Here I came; its voice
Still sounding amid the winds
And the warring elements
  Echoed to my fury.

EDG.  What wilt thou with me?

HEN.              Listen!
The vengeful sword of me
And mine, hangs o'er thy head—
Thou shalt not fall by another's hand,
Oh never!—too well thou knowest
Who shall take thy life!

EDG.  I know that o'er my father's ashes
I have sworn to pierce thy heart.

HEN.  Thou?

EDG.  When?

HEN.  At break of day.
Before the sun appears.

EDG.  Where?

HEN.  Among the icy tombs
Of Ravenswood.

EDG.  I'll be there.

HEN.  And there prepare to stay.

EDG.  There I wilt thee slay.

*a 2.*

O sun! hasten thy rising,
  Bind thy brow with a gory garland,
  To illumine the odious contest
  Of a blind fury and mortal hatred.
The infernal spirits demanding vengeance,
  Will spur our souls;

Del tuono che mugge—del nembo rugge,
Più l'ira è tremenda—che m' arde nel cor.
ENR. *parte*, EDG. *si ritira.*)

## SCENA III.

*Galleria nel castello di Ravenswood illuminata.*

Coro.          Di vivo giubbilo.
          S' innalzi un grido :
          Corra di Scozzia
          Per ogni lido ;
          E avverta i perfidi
          Nostri nemici
          Che più, terribili,
          Che più felici
          Ne rende l' aura
          D' altro favor ;
          Che à noi sorridono
          Le stelle ancor.

## SCENA IV.

RAIMONDO, NORMANNO *e Coro.*

RAI.     Cessi...ahi cessi quel contento.
Coro     Sei cosperso di pallore !
          Ciel ! che rechi ?
RAI          Un fiero evento !
Coro     Tu ne agghiacci di terrore !
RAI.     Dalle stanze ove Lucia
          Trassi già col consorte,
          Un lamento...un grido uscia,
          Come d' uom vicino a morte !
          Corsi ratto in quelle mura...
          Ahi ! terribile sciagura !
          Steso Arturo al suol giaceva
          Muto freddo insanguinato !...
          E Lucia l' acciar stringeva,
          Che fu già del trucidato ?...

The anger which rages in my heart
Is more fierce than thunder, or the tempest.


## SCENE III.

*A Room in the Castle of Ravenswood, illuminated.*

*Cho.* Let us fill
      Scotland's shore
      With joyful accents,
      For ever more,
      Our perfidious enemies
      Thus shall know
      That signally favored,
      We are prepared,
      More terrible rendered,
      And more happy ;
      That still the heavens
Smiles upon us.


## SCENE IV.

### RAYMOND, NORMAN, *and Chorus.*

RAY.   Cease, ah cease, this joy!
*Cho.*   A livid paleness covers thee ;
      Heavens ! what has happened ?
RAY.   A terrible event.
*Cho.*   Fear freezes us.
RAY.   From the chamber where
      I had conducted Lucy and her consort,
      A groan, a scream issued
      As from a dying man ;
      Thither I hastened.
      Oh, sad misfortune !
      Arthur extended on earth lay cold,
      Speechless, and bathed in blood;
      Lucy, brandishing the sword,
      Which had belonged to the slain,

Ella in me le luci affisse...
"Il mio sposo ov' è ?" mi disse :
E nel volto suo pallente
Un sorriso baleno !
Infelice ! della mente
La virtude a lei mancò !

**Tutti.**   Oh ! qual funesto avvenimento.
Tutti ne ingombra cupo spavento !
Notte ricopri la ria sventura
Col tenebroso tuo denso vel.
Ah ! quella destra di sangue impura
L' ira non chiami su noi del ciel.

**Rai.**   Eccola !

## SCENE V.

### Lucia, Alisa, *e detti*.

**Luc.**   Il dolce suono
Mi colpì di sua voce ! Ah ! bella voce
M' è quì nel cor discesa !
Edgardo ! Io ti son resa :
Fuggita io son da' tuoi nemici...—Un gelo
Mi serpeggia nel sen ! trema ogni fibra
Vacilla il piè ... Presso la fonte, meco
T' assidi alquanto...Ahimè !... sorge il tremedo
Fantasma e ne separa !
Quì ricovriamci, Edgardo, a piè dell' ara....
Sparsa è di rose ! Un' armonia celeste
Di, non ascolti !—Ah l' inno
Suona di nozze ! Il rito
Per noi, per noi s' appresta ! Oh me felice !
Oh gioja che si sente, e non si dice !
Ardon gl'incensi....splendono
Le sacre faci intorno !
Ecco il ministro ! Porgimi
La destra....Oh licto giorno !
Alfin son tua, sei mio !
A me ti dona un Dio....
Ogni piacer piu grato

Fixed her eyes on me.
My husband, said she, where is he ?
And a smile played
On her pale face ;
Hapless one !
Of reason she was bereft.

*All.*  Oh mournful event !
A gloomy terror pervades us all.
Oh night, cover with thy mantle
So dire a deed ;
Oh may that blood-stained hand
Not draw on us Heaven's anger.

RAY.  Behold her !

## SCENE V.

LUCY, ALICE, *and the above.*

LUCY  The sweet tone of his voice
Struck upon my ear ; ah ! that sound
Penetrated my heart.
Edgar, now I am thine.
I have fled thy enemy.
An icy coldness
Pervades my veins ;—
To the fountain come
And sit with me ;
A cruel phantom rises and divides us.
Didst not hear celestial harmony ?
Ah, 'tis the nuptial hymn ;
Prepared for us is the sacred rite ;
Oh happy me ; I feel a joy
Which cannot be expressed.
The incense burns, abound
The lights of sacred torches around.
See the Minister, do lay
Thy right hand in mine, oh happy day !
At last I am thine, thou art mine,
God has given thee to me ;
Every pleasure, every joy

Mi fia con te divisa....
Del ciel clemente un riso
La vita a noi darà !

Rai. Ali. e Coro.

In sì tremendo stato,
Di lei, signor, pietà.

Rai.    S' avanza Enrico !

## SCENA VI.

Enrico, Normanno. detti,

Enr.    Ditemi.
        Vera è l' atroce scena ?

Rai.    Vera, pur troppo !

Enr,               Ah ! perfida !
        Ne avrai condegna pena...

Rai. Ali. Coro.

        T' arresta... Oh ciel !

Rai.                        Non vedi
        Lo stato suo ?

Luc.            Che chiedi ?

Enr.    Oh qual pallor !

Luc.              Me miscra !

Rai.    Ha la ragion smarrita.

Enr.    Gran Dio !

Rai.             Tremare, o barbaro,
        Tu dei per la sua vita.

Luc.    Non mi guardar sì fiero...
        Segnai quel foglio è vero...
        Nell' ira sua terribile
        Calpesta, oh Dio ! l' anello !
        Mi maledice ! Ah ! vittima
        Fuì d' un crudel fratello,
        Ma ognor t' amai... lo giuro...
        Chi mi nomasti ?    Arturo !—
        Ah ! non fuggir... Perdono...

Coro.    Qual notte di terror !

I shall share with thee—
A propitious Heaven ends the strife,
Will grant us happiness and life.

RAY., ALI., *and Chorus.*

In what frightful state is she,—
Do take, O Lord! of her pity.

RAY.  Here comes Henry!


SCENE VI.

HENRY, *and the above.*

HEN.  Speak!
This atrocious deed, is it true?

RAY.  Alas, it is!

HEN.          Ah, perfidious one!
Thou shalt suffer the penalty thou dost merit!

RAY., ALI., *and Cho.*

Oh heavens! stop.

RAY.          Dost thou not see
Her state?

LUCY          What dost thou ask?

HEN.  What a horrid paleness!

LUCY          Unhappy me!

RAY.  Reason has left her.

HEN.  Good God!

RAY.          Cruel man, you ought
To tremble for her days.

LUCY  Look not on me with angry eyes!
I signed that paper, 'tis true.
In his unbounded wrath,
Oh God! he tramples under foot the ring,—
He curses me,—I have been
A cruel brother's victim,—
But I ever loved thee,—
I swear it—Arthur, didst thou say?—
Ah, fly not! pardon me.

Cho.  What dreadful night.

Luc.    Presso alla tomba io sono...
        Odi una prece ancor.
        Deh ! tanto almen t' arresta,
        Ch' io spiri a te d' appresso...
        Già dall' affanno oppresso.
        Gelido langue il cor !
        Un palpito gli resta...
        E un palpito d' amor.
        Spargi di qualche pianto
Cho.      Il mio terrestre velo,
Luc.      Mentre lassù nel cielo
        Io pregherò per te...
        Al giunger tuo soltanto
        Fia bello il ciel per me !

           RAI. ALI., Coro.

    Omai frenare il pianto
        Possibile non è !
Enr.    (Vita di duol, di pianto
        Serba il rimorso a me !)
    Si tragga altrovè... Alisa...
        Pietoso amico... Ah! voi
    La misera vegliate..
               (Io più me stesso)
    (In me non trovo !)
Rai.             Delator ! gioisci
    Dell' opra tua.
Nor.          Che parli !
Rai.    Si, dell' incendio che divampa e strugge
    Questa casa infelice hai tu destata
    La primiera favilla
Nor.          Io non credei...
Rai.    Tu del versato sangue, empio ! Tu sei
    La ria cagion !  Quel sangue
    Al ciel t' accusa, e già la man suprema
    Segna la tua sentenza... Or vanne, e trema

LUCY  I am near the grave;
      Listen to my prayer;
  Stop at least so long that I
      May close by thee here die.
      Already oppressed by grief
      Death brings to me relief.
    And if still beats my heart,
      Beats for love before we part,
    Shed a few tears.

*Cho.*  What dreadful night.

LUCY  I am near the grave,
      Listen to my prayers.
      Shed a few tears
  On my remains,
      And in heaven for thee
      I'll ever pray;
  Then, and then only, shall I be happy,
      When thou hast rejoined me.

       RAYMOND, ALICE, *and Chorus.*

  Oh! who can refrain
  From tears?

HEN.      Remorse prepares for me
  A life of woe and torments.
  Take her away.  Alice
  My kind friend, I trust to you
  To watch, on the unhappy one.

RAY.      Impious spy, rejoice
  Of thy work

NOR.  What says't thou?

RAY.  Yes thou art the guilty cause
  Of this family's destruction
  Thou didst kindle the first fire.

NOR.      I did not think

RAY.  Wretch, the blood that was shed
  It was through thee.  That blood
  Accuses thee in Heaven.  The mighty
  Hand, signs thy sentence now.  Go and fear.

## SCENE VII.

### *Le Tombe. Notte.*

Edg. Tombe degli avi miei, l' ultimo avanzo
    Di una stirpe infelice
    Deh! raccogliete voi. Cessò dell' ira
    Il breve foco...... sul nemico acciaro.
    Abbandonar mi vò. Per me la vita
    E orrendo peso! l' universo intero
    E un deserto per me senza Lucia!
    Di liete faci ancora
    Splende il Castello! Ah! scarsa
    Fu la notte al ripudio! Ingrata donna!
    Mentr' io mi struggo in disperato pianto
    Tu ridi, esulti accanto
    Al felice consorte!
    Tu delle gioje in seno, io...della morte.
      Fra poco a me ricovero
        Darà negletto avello..
        Una pietosa lagrima
        Non scorrerà su quello!
        Fin degli estinti, ahi misero!
        Manca il conforto a me!
      Tu pur, tu pur dimentica
        Quel marmo dispregiato:
        Mai non passarvi, o barbara,
        Del tuo consorte a lato...
        Rispetta almen le ceneri
        Di chi moria per te

## SCENA VIII.

### *Abitanti di Lammermoor dal castello, e detto.*

Coro. Oh meschina! oh caso orrendo!
      Più sperar non giova omai!
      Questo dì che sta sorgendo
      Tramontar tu non vedrai!
Edg. Giusto cielo! Ah! rispondete:
      Di chi mai, di chi piangete?

## SCENE VII.

### *The Tombs. Night.*

EDG.   Tombs of my ancestors, alas ! enclose
The last branch of an unhappy race—
The transient fire of anger is extinguished.
I'll throw myself on my enemy's sword—
Life is to me a burden ;
Without Lucy, the universe
To me is a desert.
The castle is yet resplendent
By the light of brilliant torches.
Ah ! too short has been the night
For festivity.   Ungrateful woman !
Whilst I am bathed in tears,       [band.
Thou art revelling in joy with thy happy hus-
Thou amidst pleasure, and I among the dead ;
   But soon will a neglected tomb
     Receive my remains ;
     And not a tear of compassion
     Will bathe my sepulchre.
     Alas, the last consolation of the dying
     Will be denied me.
   Thou, too, wilt forget
     This despised marble ;
     But come not, ingrate,
     With thy consort ;
     Respect, at least, the ashes
     Of him who died for thee.

## SCENE VIII.

### EDGAR, *and the Inhabitants of Lammermoor.*

Cho.   Oh hapless one !   Oh sad event !
     From henceforth hope has fled ;
     This dawning day will be
     Unseen by thee.

EDG.   Just Heaven ! answer !
     Who are ye weeping for ?

*Coro.* Di Lucia.

Epg. Lucia diceste !

*Coro.*   Si ; la misera sen muore.
Fur le nozze a lei funeste...
Di ragion la trasse amore...
S' avvicina all' ore estreme,
E te chiede... per te geme.

Epg. Ah ! Lucia ! Lucia !

*Coro.*                   Rimbomba
Già la squilla in suon di morte !

Epg. Ahi ! quel suono al cor mi piomba !
E' decisa la mia sorte !
Rivederla ancor vogl' io...
Rivederla, e poscia..

*Coro.*               Oh Dio !
Qual trasporto sconsigliato ?
Ah ! desisti... ah ! riedi in te..

## SCENA ULTIMA.

### Raimondo *e detti.*

Rai. Ove corri sventurato ?
Ella in terra più non è.

Epg. Tu che a Dio spiegasti l' ali,
O bell' alma innamorata,
Ti rivolgi a me placata...
Teco ascende il tuo fedel.
Ah ! se l' ira dei mortali
Fece a noi sì lunga guerra,
Se divisi fummo in terra,
Ne congiunga un Nume in ciel.
Io ti seguo...

Rai.               Forsennato !

*Coro.*   Che facesti !

Rai. *Coro.*           Quale orror !

*Coro.* Ahi tremendo ! ahi crudo fato !

Rai. Dio, perdona un tanto error.

FINE.

*Cho.* Lucy!

EDG. Lucy, said ye?

*Cho.* Yes, the hapless one dies;
Sad were her nuptials;
Through love she lost her reason;
Her end draws near;
On thee she calls and sighs.

EDG. Ah! Lucy, Lucy!

*Cho.* The bell proclaims
Her death by her peals.

EDG. Alas! that sound vibrates on my heart—
My fate is fixed.
I'll see her again—
See her, and then—

*Cho.* Oh God!
Rash thought! Take advice.
Ah, desist! be thyself.

### SCENE LAST.

RAYMOND, *and the above.*

RAY. Where art thou running, unhappy man?
She dwells no more on earth.

EDG. Thou, oh angelic soul! filled with love,
Who hast winged thy flight to heaven—
Look not on me with anger.
Let thy faithful lover come to thee.
Ah, if on earth the anger
Of mortals waged a war against us,
And kept us divided here,
Let God unite us in heaven.
I' ll follow thee.

RAY. Rash man!

*Cho.* What hast thou done?

RAY. *and Cho.* What horror!

*Cho.* Ah, cruel and fatal destiny!

RAY. May God pardon this error!


END OF THE OPERA

Lightning Source UK Ltd.
Milton Keynes UK
UKOW06n0609061215

264076UK00009B/175/P